Gypsy Horses

by Grace Hansen

Abdo
HORSES
Kids

abdopublishing.com

Published by Abdo Kids, a division of ABDO, P.O. Box 398166, Minneapolis, Minnesota 55439.

Copyright © 2017 by Abdo Consulting Group, Inc. International copyrights reserved in all countries. No part of this book may be reproduced in any form without written permission from the publisher.

Printed in the United States of America, North Mankato, Minnesota.

102016

012017

 THIS BOOK CONTAINS RECYCLED MATERIALS

Photo Credits: Alamy, Glow Images, iStock, Minden Pictures, Shutterstock, ©David Muscroft p.11 / Shutterstock.com

Production Contributors: Teddy Borth, Jennie Forsberg, Grace Hansen

Design Contributors: Dorothy Toth, Laura Mitchell

Publisher's Cataloging in Publication Data

Names: Hansen, Grace, author.

Title: Gypsy horses / by Grace Hansen.

Description: Minneapolis, Minnesota : Abdo Kids, 2017 | Series: Horses | Includes bibliographical references and index.

Identifiers: LCCN 2016944095 | ISBN 9781680809275 (lib. bdg.) | ISBN 9781680796377 (ebook) | ISBN 9781680797046 (Read-to-me ebook)

Subjects: LCSH: Gypsy horses--Juvenile literature.

Classification: DDC 636.1--dc23

LC record available at http://lccn.loc.gov/2016944095

Table of Contents

Gypsy Horses 4

Uses & Personality 18

More Facts 22

Glossary 23

Index 24

Abdo Kids Code 24

Gypsy Horses

Gypsy horses turn heads wherever they go. They are both beautiful and strong.

4

5

A group of people **bred** these horses long ago. They are known as the **Romani** people.

7

The **Romani** people moved from place to place. They had to travel with all of their belongings. Gypsy horses pulled the family wagons.

Gypsy horses were **bred** to be hard workers. The **Romani** still have great pride in their horses.

Gypsy horses are easy to spot. They have flowing manes and tails. Their lower legs are heavily **feathered**.

Gypsy horses come in many colors and **patterns**. Common colors include **bay**, white, and black.

14

Gypsy horses have short backs. Their **hindquarters** are heavily muscled. They have strong legs and large hooves.

Uses & Personality

Today, gypsy horses can do many things. They are popular carriage horses. They are also trail and show horses.

19

These horses are smart and hardy. They are also good-natured. For these reasons, they are easy to train. They are friendly toward people of all ages.

More Facts

- Gypsy horses were not always **bred** for **feathered** legs. It was not ideal because it dirtied easily.

- Gypsy horses go by many names. They are also called Cobs, Gypsy Cobs, Irish Cobs, Gypsy Vanners, Tinker horses, and more.

- There is a reason for the many names. The horse traveled to many different places. When it was traded or bred in new places, it was sometimes given a new name.

Glossary

bay – reddish brown.

bred – made to look a certain way and be able to do certain things.

feathered – tufted or fringed.

hindquarters – the rear part of an animal.

pattern – a repeated marking.

Romani – a group of people who have some cultural similarities and who move from place to place, living mostly in Europe and the Americas.

23

Index

back 16

breed 6, 10

color 14

hindquarter 16

hooves 16

legs 12, 16

mane 12

pattern 14

personality 20

Romani 6, 8, 10

strong 4

tail 12

uses 8, 18

abdokids.com

Use this code to log on to abdokids.com and access crafts, games, videos and more!

Abdo Kids Code:
HGK9275